CSU Poetry Series XL

Beckian Fritz Goldberg

In the Badlands of Desire

Cleveland State University Poetry Center

Funded Through
Ohio Arts Council

727 East Main Street
Columbus, Ohio 43205-1796
(614) 466-2613

Contents

Three

Acknowledgments

There are great longings
like someone who wakes up
in a bed in which he didn't fall asleep.

—Yehuda Amichai

One

The Possibilities

After a wife's death a man may talk
to his horse with a great tenderness
as if, just this morning, he had tried on
her pink slipper. And if he has no horse
he may crack his window a little
wider when it lightly rains to confirm
the roofs and trees are made
of paper. If there is no rain
he may make himself a meal at midnight,
sweet artichokes and Danish cheese,
a glass of red wine. If there is
no red, then white. He may suck the knife
clean with his tongue. Later

lying awake he may hear the wild lung
of a motorcycle far off on a far road.
If there is no motorcycle, a dog
trying for any syllable in any known
language. Something falling suddenly in
the closet, according to some law.

Nearness in the dark is a kind of beauty
though it is only a lampshade, a shoulder
of the walnut chair. If there is no chair,
then a shelf. A shelf of books with the devil's
violet fedora tossed on top. Or something
exotic from the sea, manta ray

like the pulse in the ball of his foot.
A man may walk ten steps behind
his life. It may be sorrow or fear.
He may see her back like two doves rushing
up where a boy has flung a handful
of pebbles. If no pebbles, leaves
where a masked prowler hunches, his belt of

lockpicks, his bag of velvet like the one
from which memory snatches. These are

the possibilities, the immaculate
like miracles which are nothing
in themselves, but in this world a sign
of angels, ghosts, supernatural beings
who watch us. Who listen. Who sometimes
helplessly let us stumble on
their pyramids, their crude observatories
or let us, generation after
generation, speak to the broken horse
of the human heart.

The Winged Eye

When I go to hell they weigh my heart.
The walls are painted with the lacquer
gaze of jilted brides. I wonder why I am here.

The devil comes, soft and cloven like a burnt cake.
He opens his manual.
It is called *How to Interpret Your Dreams.*
We sit in the garden where lips

purse in the snapdragons. A chicken
lands on his arm leaving its claw
print in his skin like creases in the cardboard
seal of a cereal box

pressed beneath a thumb.
When he reads he moves his mouth.
When he looks up he asks me if I remember
the world with swans. He

misses them most. My eye,
he says, has wings. He reminds me of
an old boyfriend who told me the greatest
men, the greatest minds in the world have

believed in God. It was much
like this. We were leaning by the river, sweet
helixes of light unhinging in
the current, and I was waiting for

a kiss. Not philosophy. And not
the devil's pining.

Love, Scissor, Stone

In April, he had forgotten where I was.
He was thinking of the stars and the police
badges deflecting little signals
where the night went down over my body
on the riverbed road. When I came back

from the dead, he was angry. It was past
midnight. He had already been rehearsing
his behavior at the inquest, already
prepared the emptiness, scoured and transparent
as a guest wing in our house. Moths

had opened a place in their burning books
for me as the headlights threw
the west wall up and its window—the one
we'd bricked and plastered over from
the inside to block the morning

scissor light. The cat clouded
two perfect jades as I came in, and the vase
was there, right there on the table,
a thickening in the water and a loose
wand of stock

had snowed around it where I sometimes
left a coffee cup, a note. I had risen
and was walking toward a place to leave
my shoes. He was in the half-light.
Or it was the sawed shadow

of that door. Once, he had wanted me
alive. We had slept in the corridors of hot
Italian trains all night, bread
in our suitcases and one-shot bottles
of brandy. But now

it was only spring. Some year. And his eyes
came flat at me, asked me where
the hell I was. I was
without a word for once, and turned

down the hall to the room of shoes,
and ashtrays, and cool cups, where I
sometimes wrap that word
around a stone.
And though I could lie

I do not. Though I could say in love
when there's not the light place there's
the buried place, that when he fell asleep
the house was breath
dovetailing breath,

I am not sure
I could believe it. There is, after all,
a life to live, not speaking, through dinner,

at twilight. I know no man or woman
plans this. It seems always
to happen suddenly, as if we've been
sleeping. Then awakened. And the smell of citrus
is curded in the night air, sour,

and too sweet. But we bear it.
Because it's here. It's where
the hell we are.

Backlight

It is the year my father stops walking and sits
on each step hoisting up with his arms
his weight to the next. His legs drag
like the necks of shot geese.
Outside, the snow rubs off
some wing of the wind. The dog
who will be put to sleep in the spring
trembles near the shed
with his left leg high, sniffs
the seal of himself on the frozen ground.

I am unmarried and do not know
how life is simplified by cruelties.
The nights glisten like fever.
My dreams hang like coral blossoms.
When I dream of falling it is always
from cliffs with my father in old
Ramblers and DeSotos from the fifties.
We sail off the edge and I die
awake, before the splintering and burning.

I come to understand how the air waits
as we leave the road and, below, the rock
and dry grasses warp everlasting—though soon
the spine of the river will snap. I come to
darkness and listen as a distant
highway drops off. The last white petal

of sound shimmies down like ice
faltering in a glass I watch
years later, about to leave
his hands.

Black Fish Blues

I've got a cigarette and a bee outside my window.
The window is dusty, speckled like an old pear skin.
I've got a cleaning woman coming once a week,
a pomegranate tree with its red bomber lips

ticking the wind quiet outside. Wind
you can see but not hear. I've got a cup
of coffee and hours the size of my palm.
A cup of coffee and the taste of muddy water

stubbing my teeth. Muddy water like the child in me
finds in her dreams. I don't know why I go there.
Bee with its striped brain loves the curl
light shaves in the air. Curl you can follow but

not see. I've got a view and a neighbor with a drainpipe
running off his roof. I've got a feel for the plumbing
broken in those shadows. I've got May light
coming in strong on all stations and branches

knocking their shadows flat on the blocks of the fence.
I've got a whole cluster of black fish bobbing
in the top block. Fish that touch you quick
constellations below the water. I remember this.

I've got a third hand and a third leg, another
skin that remembers things. I've got that leg
halfway up the road I'm walking with my sister
in the snow of '58. There's the body of a rabbit

trapped beneath the ice. There's the marble
of stillness and shadow. It's a long way
to the heart of our house. It's a long way,
sister, to here, my good legs crossed

as I sit in my chair. I've got shoes
waiting over in the corner like I've died.
Red shoes that go with nothing I own.
They've got their heels near each other

for conversation. I'm talking about being
all right when you meet yourself coming or going.
I've got a bee talking soft zeros near
the tree outside my window. I've got an eye

that can look right through. I've got a soul
full of salt like an olive. I've got a cleaning woman
who comes and touches all my things. Who raises them up
and sets them down. I've got an idea they love her

not me. I've got an idea each girl dumb like the spring thinks
she's the first and only. I've got a notion to sit here
all day and get the blues about the light
and how it will feel in ten years. I don't know why.

Sometimes the past walks right through me like an old
        boyfriend.
Sometimes the past like an old boyfriend walks
through me. I don't know if I say goodbye
or hello or drink coffee. If I answer

its question or get distracted hearing
my mother and father come in late
and drop their coats. It's spring '60.
Their dark feet swim near my door and their voices

hook on the taut line of whispers. I've got a line
on those whispers. I've got them
hushing each other, my mother and father,
coming in strong and late. They're saying

words low as wounds given under water, words
without lights on and I'm bursting to tell them
hushing each other, my mother and father,
I'm awake, still awake. Wide awake.

To a Girl Writing Her Father's Death

Sometimes the lake water writes and writes and gets
no answer. You tell me, It was just October.
That is good. His voice was full of love and laughter. Not
so good. Full of copper, jacks-of-diamonds, cubes
of honey, I could believe. But I did not know
your father. The moment when the cable snapped from
the boat has, however, its drama. Yet is not
enough. Try to understand the need out here for
gestures, wind, raw sound. Was it a spasm
of sex in the motor, light shingling
his black hair as the boat spun
on its wide iris down? Were you standing?
I know this must be painful, standing
at the edge of your white page with someone
gone under. You were sixteen and he called you
Princess, though it is a cliché to be
called Princess. And to be sixteen. Yet
I have looked at you and you are not now
much older. You could wear tiaras,
your blonde waves pure as the back
of the knee. Though you wear your carrot rouge
in clumsy circles, which makes me
love you. I have not lost a father
except in dreams. But each one has left
my mouth open. Speak. Make holy
detail. Let the water bead over you like cold
eyeballs. Let in the scream and the lining of the scream
and the prismic figure eights of oil
mad on the wake—and forgive me
for asking. You have to think of the world
which gave and took your father.
The world which asks for him now.
There's no sense writing poems unless
you see the mob: We who gather for the red
pulse of every ambulance, we who crowd

lifeguards kissing the still blue lips of
children on the beach, and murmur who
and how, hungry for every morsel
of this life that is not ours, not really. Not
for long. But for the asking.

If I Were in Beijing

I live in a fat country
with salesmen who do their own
commercials, who do not know what to do
with their hands—hang, point, hitch
a ride in the suit pocket. Usefulness
is a bitter mystery. And it is such a simple
country. Stars flag the sucked in black
hills of night. Summer stops
breathing when you listen. Or the stars are
a thousand deer tails lifted and
disappearing. You can sail down the tunnels of
radios from opera to blues. We would each

love a revolution. A better cause than just
the old dying. A priest said to my husband
the other day, "Frankly we're all sick
and tired of hearing about the holocaust."
I suppose he meant we must keep cruelty
alive to understand it. Keep it personal.
For him it's Nicaragua. The abortions.
His country where the souls of the unborn
fester like sweet fruit we do not eat.

If I were in Beijing I would be the student
facing a tank. If I were in Russia
I would be the poet in the gulag.
If I were in Argentina I would be
sewing the names of the disappeared
into my shawl and walking the plazas.
But too often I am in my own childhood,
its silent movies, its fish-thrashings of light.
Too often I am buried in the clover of the silence
of my own house. I do not know how long
it is before the dead stop counting. I hold
my breath. Each heart must find the terror
it can deny is like its own.

The Beard

The mind plays its trump:
I dream I wake up.
In the mirror I face
my face, as if to read for beauty
or for lies. Light is strong as the back
of the hand against my cheek, skin
fuzzed with flyaway hair I stroke down,
down to my chin, a brown goatee
glistening like the tassel
on a Chinese lantern. Needless
to say I despair. I am where
no thought helps. I think

of razors, scissors, tweezers, masks,
needles, wax, bleach, burning matches, drastic
measures. Spiraling explanations. The horror
of my kiss: It should go near no man. This
should happen to no woman.
I cannot stop staring, tugging at the new
part of myself as·if finally I, ordinary
citizen, were the one to actually discover
the part of the body that is the seat
of the soul. Not in the spleen or the brain
but under the chin, growing, curiously soft
like the pale mane asleep under
husks of corn. When I wake again

it is for real. My hand goes
to my face as a mother's to fever.
I am smooth, smooth in the dark as the round
stone you pick up on a walk and
hold because it feels like a remembrance.

Move Me

When I read they opened the woman
with the persistent headaches and found
in her brain a diamond
I was sure it was what I had. My ears
had been ringing for weeks.
I had blackouts the shape
of Brazil. I would come to
at parties where a stranger, shaken,
was telling me his father toward the end
begged daily, *Take me home.*
So they used to ride

for hours, miles, letting him look at houses,
children on the porches staring out
like tied balloons. Today, the sun
came up like a name
I couldn't think of last night.
I remembered

the subtle quake
of light on the hospital floor,
my father, the curtain, the man
in the bed by the door. Those nights
we'd visit, talk low beneath
the cop show sirens on TV. Each time
we'd enter or leave, each time a shadow
would flip over in the hall,
the man would whimper, *Move my arm, move
my arm.* But we could not
touch him. The cries of the old
so like gaudy valentines

from slow boys. Later the nurse drew
a chain of hushes through the curtain rings
and he whispered, *move me, move me,*

as if to a young girl bending
in his sleep. And she would
sit him up, the sheets falling
to their slow drift around his hips,
and nothing past the smooth
humps at his shoulders. Nothing.
Like a gray violin.

Beauty Sleep

Someone has just pointed out Jupiter, the smolder
behind its widow's veil of mist. In another
unfamiliar part of town I can imagine I am
anywhere, green school balanced on the black
jet of a dream. Earlier I heard two students
discovering the beauty of the open
body, the fetal pig who comes apart like
a flower, a curled thumbbook of prayer. Midnight

at the all night gas station, the phone booth lit
against oleanders, a gold door through
the back of a buddha. I do not like to
look at the sky, its weeping figs and firebirds.
Its furthest fragile nebula like the steam
of a rabbit's breath on a cracked
cellar window. In sleep, there is no sky.

There is an embroidered canopy, red-threaded
fields and beetle wings of muscled satin and
the emerald gloom of peacocks. There, the white
dog lives, and the rote bodies of the dead like addresses
remembered from childhood, names
I'll never use like *Shulamit, Cornelia, Magdalena,
Rose-Inez*. Trees as lovely and strange

as men in magenta velvet. Night deep as a wound's
heat. My sisters are stargazers. My friends
try prayer. But the sky haunts me like a sad hat
drifting down from a window. Like poems written
in dreams, their perfect sestets and blue-throated
roses, irretrievable when I wake and dawn
magnifies the hesitations of the stars, as many
as the left hand in its life, holding
what the right is used to.

The Joplin Nightingale

I share this time with a nightingale who was,
in past lives, both Scarlatti and Joplin.
—Norman Dubie, Interview

Jew's-harp in the bushes. Dark lid
on the roof. Some woman leans
unpinning her slip
from a line. It falls, the silk
white blot like a child's image

of the soul. It is the hour for devotions.
The boy with the fever knows how
night comes, the way it is
his eyes and then
it is him. The nightingale lights,

groom of the moon,
and opens. It is something like a glass
purrs to a passing plane,
this song. When I was just sixteen,
that summer, a letter came

and I read it as I walked.
Dusk, and a blind of poplars
like the giants who had the world
before us. It was simple
and expected: My grandfather

had died. And there was a train
desperate on the other side of the river
beyond the trees, carrying
wounded clarinets. Now

each time there is a darkness
and a train sounding, my grandfather
dies, and I die
for being sixteen. That is what
song does. How in this world

we become the other: the lace
bodice filled with grass. The boy
coming hot to his shadow. Like turn,
counterturn, stand. Like a love story.
Or ragtime.

Black Heart

Mist of the body out of the body:
This is the sky as winter dreams.
Our bedsheets drape the smallest
trees. The wood fence wet with its other
color. Evening. The darkness has brothers.
One is in the house,
jaw to the stove. I'm not going
in. I have in. I have out. Both
like names waiting to be lit
by remembrance, sudden, or a cry.
The name of this moment is December,
six o'clock, a few stars backed
against the distance like glances
deep into the black heart. The trees
are clothed with us, old
flowers on which we slept and
spilled. Out there, no mark
where the moon should be
pink—oh, round as absence. Then
a plume of the rain's smell,
an invisible sickness
like a minute that keeps returning.
His face strikes
in the heat of my eye. Night
is creeping into solids—earth, cold,
house, bed. Distinctions
perish. Tonight you and I will sleep
beside one another like water
and history.
His face is close
as the white of my dream.
You touch me believing
some good will come of this
but desire is all of this—
the coming and the not.

The Horse in the Cellar

The dream is still warm. Death with its butterfly
face, its eyes with iodine dropped deep in
the iris. The farm of my childhood sank
into its head like the star going out
on an old TV set. My father was a willow.
My mother was a stove. Like skin from milk
the curtains skim off the window of that
other house where they had been masquerading.
Their fold returns. And the mirror swirls its oil.

Let there be arms again. Feet. Palms.
The boat in my wall touches its blue
prow to the bed. All passengers
drowned in the crossing. I need the light, light
with a holy dove in it. But I remember
in the dark which has died and died

the last of a royal house: A child
letting the white dials of dandelions walk
her knuckles. My mother rubbing
their gold under my chin. The hens filing
themselves in the wind. The bondage
of spring: Horse in the cellar, crack
with sweet grass up to his eye.

But sleep, all memory gone on the right side,
has only the story's broken beginnings.
Once I had an uncle, a mother, a burning dress . . .

You have to die, as Aristotle said, to know
you were happy.

Two

Monsoon

The heaviness of twilight at noon. Stillness
like a thug in the wings. The sky thinks
over glass. A man stares at the telephone.
There is the moment that waiting becomes
luminous, the roundness of the air visible
as he had always guessed. He hangs in the dome
with a few green leaves. Then darkness

cinches the house up in its sack.
And you know how people think of things once
inside. Sometimes he thinks of dialing the number
that used to bring his mother's voice. Would it
ring, would it reach a woman with flour
like moon seas on her apron, string
around her finger. A reminder.
Perhaps it is connected

to the voice that says I'm sorry.
To the man who is passing the booth.
Perhaps he would interrupt a robbery or love.

The cloud smashes open like fruit.
The ozone of junipers rinsed in gin.
He thinks when the dead die, children go in
and lift the lids of the music boxes
in their rooms. They discover how jewels are places
lonelier than darkness. The rain better

than a thousand mothers.

Annunciation

If there had never been a night
in a place where a door stood half open
like a breathing thing
breathless at the moment of its arc
and light coming
from a room, its gold stick in its gold
veil, desire

could have been another thing
like sleep, or the white nervousness
of deer. And she would not have stood
behind him, her world
baroque—shot with rays of light,
Venus-clouds, fainting angels . . .

The door was half open.
At the desk he sat writing.
On his shoulder a scent curved—
cherrywood, bread at the end of the sea.
He knew nothing.

A fire of thirty wings whirred behind him.
Over his shoulder leaned
small brows of snowy everlastings.
She stood hair's-breadth
from falling, from burning her lips on
the salt of him

while he knew nothing but the room
and the text and the hour he would go
home, the way a man does at night
in a place where a door is waiting,

and the last moon
in August, brilliant in its gold sweat,
whispering: *Even in the desert*
no desire
like the desire for one

drop of you.

The Influence of Hair

For years I have kept the hair of a man
curled in a locket: Between the thumb-sized
doors of the heart, it is the yellow
of oversleeping. Now and then
I look into its slight riddle,
a shudder like toy guitars
thumped on the back. Soon those hills fan out
and then the house from their bellies, the moon,
the thin, mysterious mouth
of a man now smooth as his brother shadow, fallen,
swept under memory.
There his face has vanished like a spare key.

Yet there is even in the lost
the imperceptible fallout, the sweet
of the tongue to the empty socket,
or the sense of an unbearable dress
slipping in among the others in the closet.

Twilight. In this world how astonishing it is
not to be young. To become the four directions,
leaving, having left, reliving,

leaving. I envy what fits in my hand
inanimate and dumb, even the plainest thing,
the button from an unnaccountable bodice, from an
        unremembered
haste, or a campaign, like a decoration left after
the holiday. Maybe these are the gentle brushes
with a world that drifts like the ease of a sudden
feather, in a careless moment of the tree.

It happens, blond cousin or lover, stranger
or dead soldier, curved lockets, receipts
tongue-tied in the back of drawers, they leave

their loose ends in the darkest places
and we need to gaze at them,
to touch the one without a body,
to run our hands.

Red

The burden of all things is light.
As the stone bears its mist in the dream,
as the bay in the field its dust
of snow. The burden of the wheel

and the stake the same. And the moon's
grain-weight on the staggering night.
Below the Mill Street Bridge, air
runs the dry bed of the river, glass

spiking its plum auras. Here a woman
who broke her neck and lived began to see
colors emanating from the body,
copper of love, indigo

halos of lust. The yellow of a man
looking in a window. Tonight
you sleep—a terrible red
solitaire, carrying your red breath

like steps, like red steps . . .
and a gray apple falling
one clot of the starlight where still
our dead hold the earth

in white starched mouths.

The Future

The future is my enemy.
It holds the bones of my mother and my father
as a room holds two chairs, as a mirror
with outstretched arms that never meet.
And right now its birds are like sunspots
and its waxy trees do not even know windows.

The future is my insane boy
with naked photographs of me all over his walls,
with his telescope and his knife,
though I am no more where he is
than a grape that has filled, ripened, dried.

It knows I have already given a hand,
a foot. Knows which shirt
I will crawl into each morning. In my dreams,
it is a fish, passing me with only its left eye.

A man and woman argue in the market
by the cherries. A dog drags a red-haired
doll into the street. A man on the bus props
his violin case in the next seat like a wife.
It is a world of strange compulsions.
Sometimes beautiful as the misery of fever,

or the bodies of water walking themselves.
But the future is filing off the names from things
so that there is no way to distinguish
a flower from a lamp, a kiss from a stare.

It knows my longing like the head
rolled from the neck.

But it does not have to come,

all it has to do is wait. The summer falls
like a dagger and then a dress. Only a rustle,
my life, the sound of leaves
getting up at night to write.

One Eye

I dreamed your dead father was a pharaoh;
we carried him with gold and canna leaves.
Next, that horses would fly faster
on the round track when painted with black
cusps and glittering symbols of the elements.

The days are warm, flushed with the pollen of olives.
When I tell you my dreams you listen
with one eye—your hand keeps doing
whatever it is doing, watering, nailing,

lifting the cup. I think this is how we always
are in the world. Half out of our mind.
There's always the window
where the reverse of the television
bounces the evening news: Out in the desert

someone has been slaughtering the wild burros.
I am brushing my hair; you are reading
a crescent moon, lash of the visible.
Everything has changed unreasonably

as the face in our sleep
from the stranger to the enemy to
the dead . . . How we have stopped wanting
love, and look only for justice.

On the third night I dream
the path toward summer is worn deeper
than air touches. There, I make a sun
on the hill, and the violet circumstances
of our departure: A war, an obligation,

a flood. Circumstances under which
it is easier to see our losses
pure. A cry,
an old kiss, held like a shining
beetle between my teeth.

My Husband's Bride

The past begins to move at night.
A white peony too open from the heat
catches a soft light in its hackles
a room away from where the body, lost
from sleep like the amorous stranger,
the mental America, sits
with a little vodka turning
the stares of guests
in the wedding album. I hear
another year rustle by like the night's
one car. I put my hand through
the bed's blind side.
He is with her again. The bride
smiling where her shadow's thrown
a black water she could walk.
It's a day like spring in January,
a bloom pinned to the chest
where the body's grown back
over its life. All around our house
couples have begun to die
of a mysterious unhappiness.
Their supper tables have thinned
to wire. Their touch like jars
where a little doubt flutters.
They have disproved equation
after equation that a woman
and man traveling time can get out
young again and promise everything.
But it is not hers now.
The bride's face is like the delicate
print of the face of my thumb,
the part of me I have lost
but lost to him.

Satan's Box

When I come in late, the devil is up
writing his sonnet. He's drinking jasmine
tea. In search of a word he lifts the top
from his Russian box lined with velvet where
an io moth is spinning on a pin.
He sets aside

a child's one-eyed bear,
my mother's cloth tomato pincushion,
my father walking, blue button, black pen,
all the things I will never see again.

I take advantage of the commotion,
peer over his shoulder where the i's are
dotted with pentecostal hearts. It starts:
Remembrance is a fire in a drawer, ends:
Your house will melt on hinges like a star.

A Cloud is Down

The apples have locked themselves in,
rose, white, and planetary. The sky's
two blackbirds fly like before
and after. Smoky as the flesh

the old summer rises
unbraiding its arms. If there is light
in everything, everything
burns. The knob, the shingle, the bite

of edges all over the house. In the water
one long white thread is trying to catch
itself. A cloud is down. Through the neighborhood
stray dogs try to fit in but stick out

like new shoes. Yesterday you said
one thing, today another. All down

the street the doors cannot shut out
the incense of near rain. Behind them
men and women are talking things over.
He is saying, Go back
where you came from. And she is saying,
And where is that.

Adam

Crushed the first time
in the heavy hand
of mud, he hung
upside-down among the nurse
stars, and ached

like the last
plum of that first summer.
He wanted
the Angel of Morphine,
her mouth open
on the void. Each day, yes,

was forever. Heaven
held his leg by a hook.
He found he was subject
to Laws. Principles.

They took his water
in bags. They brought him
flowers. He could see light
condense to touch
the throat of the vase.
The nothings
I would use to turn him, head

over heel, in the next life.
But there, in desire's swoon
he watched small cattle throb
the earth, and the wrists
of the rivers.
Then the blackout.

I see it in his eyes
when he walks past me, the flash
of a pin in his hip: The dream

of rabbits hanging in the trees,
the tufts of the body,
and the bone
purple, jutting
from the paradise
of the lost.

Eve

Shadow between his lips sharp
as a whistle—she waits for it
to drop. In the dream
she is building a man
each hipbone in her palms,
two stones to anchor
the tent. And she anchors.

I know her in the daylight.
How her voice leaves a place,
a fluttering cymbal beneath
my breast. I examine her
hands, and put them in
my hair which last night's birds
never leave. It is dark:

Nothing is finished.
On the other side
of the body, an eye
missing, or a breast or a bone.
Only the mystery of shoulders
and instead of the face
a seam. What sleep joins,

what longing has sundered, this
is the vision of the flesh.
Night, there is no garden.
There is only us, only the stoned
flower of the mouth,
maidenhead. The swallowing word.

Can't Anyone Untie Us?

¿No hay quien nos desate?
—an etching by Goya

They are roped to the tree,
the man and the woman.
Something is wrong with the family photographs.
They are roped to the tree like two winds.
There is a picture of my body next to his body
feigning sleep . . .
They are roped to the tree like two winds who want—
one, the north, one the south with its bad
blue bruise and spunky ions of
the gulf. This afternoon we have all come
to April and stopped. We stand in the museum and we are
museum: Last year your woman left you.
Last night, another man tried to loosen me
like a flower that's been sweet too long to cling
much longer. Beside us, gazing, the Portuguese girl
you drank with until morning has forgotten
she confessed how long the married can sleep
apart in the same house.
And you feel how fiercely your hands are tied.
What distractions twist desire: The man
is bent lower than the branch, his fist
pushed against her hip, so that the rope bites
heat into her flesh and her hand goes up
and is snuffed in the wing-pit of the horned
owl stepping from the tree onto her hair.
We walk out wet as ghosts in the sun.
Our cab driver says it's five minutes before
his first beer. He's going to the roof
of the highest hotel to watch some world, the blue
bay pushing off the earth only so far . . . as if
bound by being water to being. It's a passion
in our own image: What makes us come

to what is from what mists in our troubled
hearts, in our dream-sweat. Here, where the days are
made thick and hot—
we belong, we suddenly belong to our lives
without mercy, like a sex. Tear up
all the wedding photographs. Flight ends.
Hearts change. But a woman and a man
can't pull apart without admitting the light
they made was mud and what honey they sucked
was wax and that the best they were
was nothing: Space
cleaved to the root. And even then the terrible
blank we want to fuck and fuck away
surrounds us, encircles us, puts its arms
around us—oh, we are dumb and delectable—
the ocean swaying like trees and little lies,
and waking in the garden, the *who* and *whose*
of wiser birds force down the dark
that holds us under—until we promise . . .

for R.A.

Say

Tongue, what are you doing up there in space
among the tunnels of birds and the about-to-snow,
still as the blush on far fruit?

I stand with only breath in my jaws, the absurd
fur on which I cannot place even a
finger. Then it comes to me to say about
the weather, something, by which I mean. And
he says about the weather, and I some
thing about his coat, by which I mean

everything. But he lets it drop.
Everything, what are you doing out there,
out there? Come in
like salt. But at twilight cold red lilies

half undress the spheres
inside them. Crows are snipping *want want want—*
the neighbor's broom against the walk tears out
of a terrible throat
confessions. Each time I am near
him, my voice fades like a scent. And his eyes

say, What are you doing here?
Longing is tighter than anything.
They fix to the air to the left
of my face, a black language. *And it*
about him—he is what
by which I mean by.

The Exact Address

A fire dreams of the taste of my house.
Strange nights
I sit with my hand in my hair.
Now I'm sure

this hour, this April, this neighborhood
is the exact address of desire. Yes,
a thrush tears three
crystals from its throat

the pitch of water. The moon's small,
a fist of wind in a gown.
I tell you there is no red at night
and in the roses only a place
where the eye blows out.

You once said when we die
we will be everything: The fence and the trees
and the stars and the people we have loved.

So many years ago I crossed
a street in a city whose name I can't remember,
for a meeting I can't remember.
There was a eucalyptus rowing
in the streetlight, a hundred pale
thumb studies of the face.

Already I have become
the woman in the Song of Songs
who asks, Have you seen my love?
And her love has gone
down into the garden of almonds.

When the past rises it is nothing,
smoke without flavor.

But swallowed, it was salt to raw gods.

Letter to My Twilight

Pinwheels wind their eyes in the garden.
A spark clicks its lips in the gray cat.
I do not know how to console you. I see
your mouth wrinkle like the seam of a fig.
I have seen you swinging like an angel on a hook.
I have seen the celestial X across your door.
I am the mother of your death.

Today the lost purses
of yesterday's rain unclasp in the air
the scent of citrus, soap, and honey. Spring
simply undoes me,
like a crazy lover. As it does you

brown petal of me now. I fear your mind going
pisswater instead of memory. I fear you like
the thief, noise. I want to steal

everything. But I am good
and will die. So I am writing now
the love letter now is—
promise me

something more than
flatulence and bone. Promise me you will not die
in this room. It is spring and the mail truck
idling on the street, forgetting its name.

I am good. Invent you like the bomb
and pray you will never burn.

The sky moistens with darkness. Remember
how to lie awake at night, a thread
for catching. How from up under
the silence sometimes a bird blue-noted,

then another. A sudden simmer in the bowl.
Promise me

you will not be like the others. It is a spring
so deep I lie on its tongue.
Let the blessing be a few words longer . . .

Stay in your garden. I am coming.
Though I will not know how to console you,
shadows hooped to your ankles, rooms
of a thousand cats.

I have seen your eye hanging like a spider
from the eaves after rain.
I have heard you pacing beyond the locked door
during love. On a night so alive
faces of the dead
promise me

you will read this. Because today the light's
in love and proposes to anyone.

The Drunken Hand

I steal the red car
and crash the shadows
those bandits of the dream
who guard desire.

But the roads crook,
as wine spilled on lace, and the wind
sends its rack of dresses
down the hills

and I cannot find you,
like the drunken hand cannot
find the mouth. My body
has broken into the city

of sirens and wrong hearts
and has come back
in autumn, lying
on the bed, my thick

book of psalms
where I am written
and you cannot read me
though I say, *O my love,*
my dove,
my sun.

The Widow Map

Umbrellas are made of palm fronds
on the beach of Ixtapa. Shadows
whose black clocks tell nothing.
And in Fiji the flowers sink deep
in their red suds, a boy's eyes
lift light like a toast. Widows
on cruises discover these things,

widows with money and sad girlfriends,
widows with bodies smeared like morning,
widows who let the glass of wine
walk through them, who notice the hands
of young officers their finest hairs
against white cuffs. The sea

near Jamaica is a rare blue tea.
The sea has a dream of sorting
her husband's thousand socks.
He is still green with a jaundice
the embalmer could not cover.
The widow Maria keeps a needle

in the hem of her dress. The widow
Helen wears cologne from the bottle
his cheek sleeps in lightly. Sarah Jean
eats olives and garnishes and double
plates of sweets, marbling her body
until the awful space embraces her,

pear sleeping deep in numb honey.
The nut groves on Hydra
are like the click of slow fans
in late summer. The night far out

at sea, a pure darkness with no
islands, no sleeve, no skirt.
Without emptiness, nothing moves.

Without going, no grace.

Resolutions

When I die in spring
I think of the wasp's lonely earring
above the pool in summer,
and when I die it is
summer with the first chill
of a wine glass,
its invisible writing, and I
am about thirty again, watching
the good heart of October. So

it is true: I can't imagine death
falling in any known time
of the year. Now it is

January and I have promised my mother
to write my resolutions.
I do not resolve to clean cupboards.
I do not resolve to give up
drink. Or the biting of nails.

I am afraid of promises to myself.
I hope I will be happy
in the summer, reading by the sea
feeling the blue stop
at the top of my book.
Wearing sandals.

There is, maybe this year, maybe
the next, one day that is promised
to me. On that day
I will be thinking of another

like the bride beneath the dullard
the matchmaker chose.

Three

In the Middle of Things, Begin

Bees rode the scalloped air of the garden.
The table, glazed bowls set for the afternoon meal,
trembled. A woman flashed in the archway
clutching her jewel box and an infant,
shoving them into a cart. The sleep was over.

I am near the mountain when you wake me,
the darkness ancient as the tongue
in a stone. You had slept a few hard hours
and then did not know where you were.
Small room on the Italian coast, it is strange
to us. I hear you touch things. I put up

my hand. I say *here, here*. We still
love each other. But this was years ago.
In the morning, we wander the ruins
of Pompeii, rooms cracked by golden
broom flowers, dry mosaic of a pool where
blind boy Cupid stands, the limed

jet in his loins. We step inside
the tepidarium, pale corruptions of pipe
and wall, and circle slowly the people
of ash, molded to their moment behind
museum glass. Cocooned so perfectly
in the postures of death, their bodies

tire us, even the dog's legs curled
to the tickle of stillness, torso
torqued almost playfully. We forget
it was the cloud they died from, not
the burning, not the fire. But the gray world.
Woman lying with her knees drawn up, cheek
resting on her hands. Man with his head

turned, hands flat, arms bent like a mantis
as if to push away the kiss of earth.
I am remembering them now in the middle
of things, like the married in their
separate, fitful sleep. Suffocation
and climax: Same slow drag of the mouth. Same
gouged bread of the face.

The Ecstasy

As if bone spilled
down the stairway of a long night
her marble dress unfolded the seven
sevens of light. We had come
to see the saint. And on a weekday,
only a few of the penitent
in the back pews kneeled, old women
with the blue of sin already
seeing through their hands. It was the arrow
through the heart, the hundred butterflies pinned

by one pin—the moment that was always
woman in the stone. I'd come with the girl who saved
her butter from lunch to eat later on the train,
who talked to her Jesus in her sleep. She
was twenty-five and no man had ever loved her, ever
would. She stood transfixed as if the place
is white, where joy is, and then began
to giggle, pointing

low where a skeleton lay in gold
and lilac vestments behind the glass. Its hair
the dull of hemp against the pillow. "Look,"
she said. "Look at the doll." I saw the face
of the dead, face where the devil's bear had sucked
all the honey from the comb.

Yet as this was, after all, a church and we
were strangers, and this was Italy, bright summer,
I touched the girl, felt the quiver of her shoulder
and it almost took
like a laughter from the next world
or that sadness in sex

until she turned, one iris more astonished
than the other, as if the right eye were always
far away: An age, another country, and like
the blue that is a pomegranate in its dreams.

Leda

I wanted to be like blindness in the river.

That morning the tight hum of cicadas
snapped into a fine silence. I cut
my finger on a reed, sucked
the little salt of myself as I let
the garment fall. *Something in the air,*

I might have said, as old men before
a fire, a battle. I walked the mouth
of river mud, thick lips of those Nubian
boys in sleep, then turned suddenly half
expecting their wild eyes and giggles.
I had a stone. But there was only the flat

wineskin of my shadow, and one cloud
beating with light which followed me,
my hips threaded with water
as I floated back, my skull light
in the bell pull of my hair.

When the first feather struck
I remembered the slave girl's stillborn,
its melded hand, its hole for nose,
its sealed eyes. We buried him shallow
in a grove of aleppos. This
is not the god's story—it is mine.
It is not straight. It is how the swan

warped my shape in his, like the second
ring of water the first. He moved
like a way, not a thing: All
hypothetical particles, shuddering
W's and Z's. And it was breath first

I fought for through the creature's weight
heavy with the odor of musk, of cumin.
My nails sank into the tender edge
of thunder. Rabid snow. He shoved
his hard comb into my hair, and wasted
me with light. I am the leper whose heart
falls out first. But when I rose,

at last, from the river
in the thousand drops of my skin
I was boiling. I was a woman . . .

I do not want to be one with anything.

Moon in Adolescence

The mothers in this town have
daughters who've gone crazy, slipped
out like radical angels through
a hole in the roof. And tonight
the glimmer of winter
where the streets stub out
is all that's left. The girls
with their eyes made up like scorched
blossoms, have drifted off
as boys to sea, to war,

but without the sea, without
the war. They dig their lovers'
names with a crude knife on
the inner eclipse of thighs, for
what they are after is
a personal sadness, the throbbing
cult of heat. The mothers sink

back from their windows
fathomless as silence and Thursdays.
And somewhere a car
motor won't won't won't
because this is madness,
trigger season—the raving
of eggs light as goldenrod,
wheat, until the stars are a field
of dogs with their tails
on fire, bitches

tearing off to birth.

Eros in His Striped Shirt

I decided to stop
meeting my demons, detoured
that street, that orchard full of yellow
spheres that never revolved, and went
around the stairs where—

This is delicate.
There are things you should not say
because you love someone.

I woke many nights. The last
suddenly like a beat
in a drum. Demon *If*. *If*
with his black beard and his
brown coat, gazing down at
me from the stairs. How I followed him,

schoolgirl.
Do you imagine at night someone
going to bed the very moment
you are going to bed? Turning
out the light?
And isn't it so quiet you swear
the heart is telepathic.
Isn't it—

I came out of myself like fire
and went back in. We do
lose what we never had. Because
we imagine.
(A dangerous imagination, Mother said)

As if in a library—
as if on my naked shoulder—
they whisper *Yes, we are horses*

and offer the beggar's ride.
But I've done to me and I've done to me.
(Out of control, Husband said)

Now I'm on foot, dragging
the mind's clandestiny.
(You will meet the ministers
but not the Prince, I *Ching* said)
Night's floored it to the metal,
ruinous obsession. Flesh, beware—

to live is homesick.

Nocturnal Epilepsy

The child wakes inside a clock.

Two tongues of light up to his eyes, already
his foot where darkness is a polish
dances the moon-gear on the floor. She
sees him in his cool pajamas, jerking,
the nerve in the lamb the slaughterman
can't stop. The first time

not knowing what it was but late, and
spring, and her own son waving her off—
fiend she-pendulum with a face
from his spider book—she stood calling
his name, calling though he looked

right through the wave of it, pupils fixed
where a name sometimes washes up, bone,

on the other shore. She slept on the edge
of his bed for a year, nights he'd glow
suddenly, spark even through her arm
to the fringe of epilepsy. And other nights
whole nights blown blond with his body,
a sapling stripped white, a leg

out of the moon. Quiet.
She looked up from a nighthawk's
ink in an etching, and twenty years
were gone. Her room before midnight hanging
leafy blue and then, toward dawn,
a just blue. The bird an earshot.

Nothing is more binding than the night.
Orange blossoms wreck the air.
She sees him dancing, boxing

the upright dream. A shadow
in whom only the subject of touch continues:

She is holding her son like a breath
from her life that brings home

her life.

Glory

The gardener shears a brown knot
of phlox and glances
toward the open window. Upstairs
the old woman is listening again
to Godfrey's recording of Roosevelt's funeral,
sighing, "He was a great man." The soft bell
of a lily rolls off into the gardener's
cuff. It's time to leave

but my fingers keep tracing
a chip in the wall. She does not know
what year it is, but that it's spring
and someone in the garden answers
to *Thomas* as her husband
used to, though he is from San Juan

and someone else's son. I bring him
a pitcher of water from the kitchen.
I feel it yawing to my walk, trying
to speak. He showers black
soil from a bag around the bushes,
Crimson Beauty, Arizona Rose.
We hear the puff

of brakes as the train slows
carrying the body of the President.
For her the war is nearly over.
Here, the gardener teaches me Spanish.
Agua, he smiles. *Las flores.*
Beso. He winks. He fingers
a button on my blouse.

He loves everything about America.

The old woman comes out and stares
from the porch, head cocked, as if hearing
music. I wave. But she bends
near the railing to the faithful
morning glory, deep of blue heels
sunk in mud. The loose things
in her memory which is great

like the age.

The Dead Are Faithful

Yes, but not to everyone they knew.
—Marina Tsvetayeva

This is the smallest window in my house,
night the size of a Bible. Naked
I stand with the shadow's basin, the graphitic
violet of the mirror, as among equals.
I have already forgotten a world,

a vague tango of green and a table
where a stranger out of my head held
my wrists. This world is still. Beyond
detection. But in the window a sudden
bare bones of light—the lion cloud—
lavender of my thigh and then—
no light. No sound.
It is as if there is no year

just the sky patch seesawing like a photograph
to the floor, a woman who has slipped
where death, in its plumb solitudes, straightens
the air, the lie that covers
another: Night again, always night,
and always me. The body

is alone with its heart and muscle,
its hands like an old clock where the bird
no longer springs through the shutters
on the hour. In the six months he mourned her
my father-in-law once confessed
he had dreams of her body beneath
the ground and maggots lit
like a fire in her face. No doubt

the years we spend in love do exist
then do not. There's the breath
my shoulders feel tonight when I bend
and drink directly from the faucet,
and my mouth runs. The storms
this summer come late and heavy like shame.
The thunder of two times falling apart.

My Sister Fear

When a plane throbs at night above the house
I imagine I am passing over myself.
But down there's the past
and I'm a prisoner like the moon
that blooms over a pool. Just beyond
those trees is the doctor's house.
Then the widow who lives with three dogs.
And so on. And just beneath the faint
lines of my face is a young girl and
an old woman, like a dolphin and a lizard
who love each other, but can't change.

Sometimes I look out
and see those who are gone, sitting
like plums in the striped chairs
on the patio. Yes, I was the one
who carried your mother's wig
to the mortician's door, the day
before her burial. I do it always. Always,
like a faithful dog. For what we're told

about time is not true.
Even in the life where I am a fisherwoman
in Wey Province, the same void
dances before me, the horizon
white as the seam through the hair.
I imagine I am looking out for myself.
You turn in your sleep and love my sister
fear, her bald shoulder, skin
with its own thin atmosphere, a life
impossible on earth.

Victorian Men

At night they drink port the shade
of lamb's blood in firelight. The pale
fiddleheads of smoke bloom, lose
their binding. Late, while it rains, and the horses
slick like lacquer near the lamppost,
the library fills with the sadness of government
but they are assured, calm. Edward, Matthew,
George, Hugh. Each has a mad sister

who has undergone the leeches and learned
the places where the skin rings, registers
surprise. She moves lightly as tea in silver
carried slowly up a stair. She dreams
the clocks walk at night and want
to mount her. In her little book

there's a ribbon sewn to the spine to keep
her place: *M. visited last evening. Wore*
the brown dress. Today a fox-eye in
the tower of an iris. No one in the garden.
Someone watching.

Not a word about the farms collapsing.
Not a word about reform—the usual
after dinner talk. And then nothing left
but the umbrellas which each man
stands under like his own church
until the hansom comes near with its desire

to rock him like a *pasha* in the gin-sweet
fog of town. Each has a wicked mistress
who hurts him dearly, slits him down
like a mouth upright in the heart
of a lily. Each night

has a room that is another
century, and always evening. Late,
its lamps blow out with the flutter
of fins. Men crawl into
the childhood of the dark, bed
with its polished monkey claws. They lie

tonight between us while it rains,
believing all the old things.
Around us the drumming of the wet earth
is the same sound as the crowd
the dead make
coming down their endless hill
in the worst of times.

The Year One

The house snuffs out like a candle in wine.
Not a light, not a wire, not a hum lives
but only the woven darkness of the street
and the rent darkness of the tree. We have lost

our century. What to do but arrive
in the underworld of the window, pale,
half-undressed, like an ancient people
sealed with their bowls, their chairs . . .

Outside, the sky trembles
from its green nightmare.
It feels like the year one.
As my mother used to say, . . . *since*
the year one, and so explain the way
things continued to happen.

It was just yesterday
we were driving through low clouds
in the hills, through cattle land
near St. David, when a woman stood in the middle
of the highway, touching
her own face. A few cars had slowed, unsure,
and a truck swerved to the red
mud of the shoulder. What her story was

we couldn't know as she slowly, barefoot,
stepped as if tranced by the shadow
in that stranger's truck:
A bad lover, bad husband, bad wine or, who knows,
just a day when everything seemed lost

and the night would come anyway
with its men and women falling silent
because the thunder
reminds them of their childhood,

and their childhood of where they are going
and what has been this way
always, and they wondering always
why it has been this way.

Narcissus

The flowers were always like faces
at the water, like blood
unable to stand
on their own, blue flowers
always wanting to be inside
but who are outside

like the faces of girls who doubt
they will be beautiful.
In a world, beauty is nervous,
on edge, the blue jet that won't
leave the flame

but huddles, mouths, attenuates,
wants to die with something.

I am sure Narcissus was not a boy
but a woman,
the way I am sure hunger
is not a dog but a goat,
and when she came to the river she

saw the face with the stone
in it, and the weed
swaying down where the water
had a mind
the way love has a look:
Fish like an arrow.
The stitch it puts through
the heart.

The Lives of the Poets

The palms rustled like torch rags
where the sky blew out. There was a half-moon.
Behind us the old hotels clung
to the strand of beach only by the nerve
of their neon, a blue, a concentrating pink.
Out there, ocean brooded like a magnet.
The air was good like chains.
It was simple: We could step off
America itself. Someone

stashed a cigarette in the sand.
And the night came after it. Bloomed
from our eyes. When we passed the breakwall
there was an old woman perched there,
dress hiked up on her plump knee, face
tilted in the stiff moon of her hair. And
the old man, standing, crushed
into her with the kind of kiss
that shamed us by its randy glory

and resurrected us in hunger.
When we stood later letting the waves
salt our ankles, just far out enough
to feel where the world goes soft,
the length of the shore was only shadow,
breeze hummed with the odor of fish.
Two of the men stripped down and swam out.
The women waded, torn. My mind

was the nude glistening out of this—
all we wanted of darkness
was for the wanting not to leave us,
the burnt eternal
pawing us with its last warm breath.
And it was almost midnight

when we took the last good look,
turned into the streets saying
we should all write
a poem about this, waiters lit
in the windows of hotel kitchens,
some traffic, and the drugstore's bricks
spray-painted with Spanish gang names and

that one American and primal word.
It was red as a thing split open.
A valentine. And we paused, waiting
at the corner as if this were no place
to end, remembering how empty
sweater sleeves draped her shoulders,
how her ankles locked and lifted
and he buried his face in her neck.
And he held her, sagging and all,
the black gulf behind them going all the way—

The Incubus

Dusk comes off on my hand,
a blue fix. The first house
to light on the street changes
everything into its evening order.

It is not mine. The heavy
oleander feels for its sight,
the lips of the darknesses
part. I go in.

I turn off the sound and let
the image flicker. Soldiers
in the desert discuss the probability
of war. I sit in the quickening
kisses of their silence

and I see you, the dream
in the middle of my life.
And I forget my life.
Like the woman entering
a room, stops
and can't remember why:

Everything appears in order.
I can't discuss
the improbability of desire.
I can't explain the light
that is always on.

I will simply never sleep again.

Sometimes your dark eyes have
the rings of the animal whose
wariness is other light.
Sometimes you are the demon who

rises from the back of the stranger
and rocks my breath . . .

I want to have no heart.
To be trained like the soldier.
The old world of my childhood—
where we died at night
like God.

Lullaby

Tonight someone keeps playing a polonaise
and stopping in the same place,
then slowly, as if spelling, repeating
the way, then pausing and

only the fringe of silence swaying.
I must drink his same drops
of milk, over and over. I begin
to think he is the devil, up late.

Behind his ear,
a pencil and in his teeth, a rose.
Tonight I dream my window
has floated open to a square

with one fountain, the falls of a stone
lion who is the blunt look
of wakefulness. Just
as I come to the feeling

I am about to name the place
I am bothered by dogs' voices snatching
back the street, my room along it,
and sad people wading the black steppes

of the piano and horses milling
a white mist, having given away
all their money.

In the Badlands of Desire

If there is the statue of a saint
whose toes are worn smooth from old women
kissing, if there is an animal whose name
is sleep, if there is a hill
whose bones are broken, I
will remember me in the next life.

If there is an onion with the hundred
smaller and smaller faces
of wet light, if there is a mirror
whose shoulders drift
the museum of shoulders,

there is a spider like a a dud star
which catches the empire
from table leg to corner, if there are communists
and useless lingerie, and rubies
snatched at night from jewelers' windows,
I will be the butcher's white

paper, the hook raving in frost.
If there is a tongue still moving
toward its mother silence, mint still breaking
its unimaginable green fist
through old aqueducts where the drunk

meet to be lonely and violet
as nets sieving the shine of nothing,
if there is a plaza in a town
where the stones break out
like hives from the plaster, and pigeons
blow their cool oboes of love,

I will be the look given to a door
when it closes by itself. After

it closes, wondering
was it some hand, some wind. And if it is painted
blue, like the faded crepe of old hours, if
a wolf bares its teeth to its tail
on the doorstep, there will be a hard winter,
a demon spring.

Acknowledgments

Grateful acknowledgment is made to the following publications, in which some of these poems have previously appeared.

The American Poetry Review: "Monsoon," "The Widow Map"

The Black Warrior Review: "Black Fish Blues," "The Winged Eye"

Crazyhorse: "In the Middle of Things, Begin," "The Possibilities," "To a Girl Writing Her Father's Death"

The Gettysburg Review: "Glory," "Move Me"

Hayden's Ferry Review: "Adam," "Backlight," "Eve"

The Indiana Review: "Beauty Sleep," "Moon in Adolescence"

The Journal: "Annunciation," "The Horse in the Cellar," "The Lives of the Poets"

Michigan Quarterly Review: "Leda"

Passages North: "The Joplin Nightingale"

Ploughshares: "The Ecstasy"

Poetry Northwest: "Black Heart," "The Dead Are Faithful," "The Future," "In the Badlands of Desire," "The Influence of Hair," "Letter to My Twilight," "Love, Scissor, Stone," "My Sister Fear," "One Eye," "Resolutions"

Sojourner: "Eros in His Striped Shirt," "My Husband's Bride," "Say"

The Virginia Quarterly Review: "Satan's Box"

Zone 3: "The Beard," "If I Were in Beijing"